love, life, and language

love.

What is Love? Love is broken down into four main types. First we need to identify the types of love, to determine which type of love we give and want to receive.

Eros: erotic, passionate love.

Philia: love of friends and equals.

Storge: love of parents for children.

Agape: love of mankind.

What does love mean for us?

Eros.

Eros is one of the most common types of love. We know this from the term 'Lovemaking'.. Funny how people that are even atheist scream, "Oh My God" during moments of ecstasy. Just a hint at the origin of love. And while we're speaking origin stories, understand that HATE only exists AFTER a failure of love. Meaning you can't Hate anyone that you've never loved. Usually hatred comes from resentment based on love not working how you want it to. Eros is the romantic love, characterized by affection, touch, and passion.

Philia.

Philia has been called the "brotherly love". It's a love that shows affection minus a romantic part. The city of Brotherly Love, Philadelphia, gets its name from the word Philia. It's characterized by deep conversations, support, openness and trustworthiness.

Storge.

Storge is the most natural-occurring love we know, other than the love God has for us. It is the love from parent to child. It's one that most of us have or will experience when having a guardian experience. It's that kind of love that allows forgiveness, even when the transaction doesn't always warrant an immediate forgiveness. It's Storge that makes us forgive acts that our children commit against us, yet the same love that urges us to create a system that teaches our children not to make the same mistakes.

Agape.

It is said that Agape is the type of love that God has for mankind. And in order to give Agape, there must be a renewed heart within the acceptance and love of God in your life. Meaning, you won't understand Agape until you've made God your Lord AND Savior, then experienced Holy Matrimony.

love, **life,** and language

Emotional Intelligence.

We equate Emotional Intelligence as the cognitive ability to discern what others are feeling.   That is true, however, there's more to EI than perception of others feelings. There's also a skill to understanding how you're affected emotionally by circumstances and making sure you exercise good judgment. Making intelligent decisions based on emotional reactions.

IF The Shoe Fits.

Have you ever met someone and thought they are YOUR TYPE? Whether it be a spiritual, physical, or mental type, we often categorize others as a good fit, or a good enough fit. Would you then wear inappropriate shoes because they're your size?   Would you wear a stylish shoe that doesn't fit well?   Let's start making sure the people we allow are a perfect fit!

Reaffirmation.

Often we put sticky notes on the mirror to remind us, or as a reaffirmation to who or what we are. The sticky note is a flag!

Nothing should have to remind you of who or what you are, and if you lose who or what you are, are you really that? You never have to be reminded of your height or race, so why do you need reminding of your character?   Or are you using the Reaffirmation as a crutch to justify your actions or feelings?

Did you react to a situation incorrectly? Is that why you posted the sticky note? Are the reaffirmations a way of you ignoring situations that you should have corrected? Do you need the sticky note to tell who you are when you're not actually being that person?

Flag On The Play.

Have you ever dated and noticed Red Flags? Yellow Flags? I'm sure you have, and at times we ignore these flags for our own personal reasons. As you grow in maturity you should consider how many flags you ignore and the value of those flags. They tend to represent issues that you cannot change or fix. Be very aware that flags are there as a warning, and they shouldn't be passed by so easily.

Random Vibes.

Try a new recipe, take a ransom trip, go on a random date.

Sometimes the randomness can be exactly what the doctor

ordered for a relationship. Always keep finances in mind, but create a random vibe within your relationship. It keeps things from becoming monotonous. You'll be surprised by the surprise when done right! Don't be afraid to create a random vibe.

Love The Signs.

Does your partner have an activity or job that they absolutely love? Whether it pays a lot, a little, or nothing at all? Oftentimes you're watching then I'm their purpose. And rather than remove them from their purpose because it doesn't suit your needs, nurture that process and see how communicating with them regarding that activity could possibly yield the results YOU seek.

For example, your spouse plays video games often, and communicates how it may be possible to earn income in several ways while enjoying that game play. Spouse likes to fish?

Encourage professional fishing. Spouse loves makeup?

Suggest creating tutorials or classes. We can't be so self

centered that we ask an entirely different person to achieve OUR

goals, especially when our goals can be achieved their way.

Encourage your mate, nurture your love, Love The Signs.

Can't Buy Love.

Love isn't buying your spouse or girlfriend a new bag. It's not

about finances at all. Love is addressing needs, often without

provocation.

Can't Force Love.

I've heard women demand to be proposed to or saying they don't have time to waste. And as a man that did not marry any of the women that provided that same pressure, I'll explain why I didn't. When men choose marriage, it's not a conscious decision. It's more of an urge. That urge is supplied by God. I believe that because of all the relationships I've been in, I've never felt this feeling before and I saw blessings immediately from my union. A man knows when he's met his mate and that urge pushes him to propose engagement or elope. You see the qualities you want in your mate then you push forward and work towards figuring out small issues. It's not because your partner 'completes you', or they look good on paper, or because you have children. It's because you get that feeling that this is your mate. It doesn't take years to know, very little time actually. It does take years to perfect the balance in the relationship. So many marriages fail early because they were married for the wrong reason or they didn't spend the time to get the balance. It's often a large adjustment to go from living single to knowing you'll only be single again if your spouse dies. Frankly, I think it's more terrifying to be old and lonely! So to those waiting to be proposed to, don't rush! Be honest with yourself and to your partner. Would you deal with yourself?   If the answer is no, then why not change how you are? Or allow your true mate to find you, single! If you're looking to propose, you don't have to ask yourself if you're ready. Just picture yourself doing it. And allow God to tell you when, it is Holy Matrimony, right?

Deciphering If This Love Is Real.

Often we use literature such as Love Languages to keep the flame going. We try to understand what makes a person 'tick' in order to keep feeding them what THEY think they need to feel love. But how often is 'honesty' labeled as a Love Language? Can't say that I've seen a person add Honesty to the things they want, and if they did, what would be the boundaries? Real love is beyond a mechanical movement to buy flowers, pay for expenses or say I Love You. Real love exists when anger is present and you still care. But let's not be foolish about it. There are times when you do things in the name of love, and you still get the short end of the stick. Does that mean that the love was any less? I would think that you learned from that love. You learned how to love someone, even though they may not be the spouse for you. At times we experience love, that's sort of practice for the right person. Sometimes we learn longevity by being with the wrong person for years. Sometimes we learn patience by loving the wrong person for some time. These are all skills you need for YOUR SOMEONE SPECIAL. Endure through, but if you don't have that urge to marry, don't. And be

honest and upfront with that person. They may feel the same.

Sustaining Love.

Often something we ask ourselves. How do we make it last? I

feel LOVE isn't a substance that we should try to stretch to last.

It's a renewable resource that we can make with one another.

Often we see love in a person and try to siphon Love from that

person without creating any to share. It looks like a smile on that

person's face that gives confidence or like the feeling from a new

haircut or wardrobe. But if we took the time to create love with

someone I think we'd cherish it more. Create those moments

that mean something to you. Create that intimacy that

supersedes other non important agendas. When was the last

time you had to pull yourself away from a person?   That usually

applies to food, sleep, or comfort.   There's a 'chemistry' that we

speak of when there's a connection.   How often do you nurture

it?   Or do you allow the other person to nurture while you wait

expectantly? Sustaining isn't the answer, creating more is.

Long-term relationships are the best example of situations where

love has to be naturally manufactured for years.   And it's

possible, but requires commitment to the idea.   It's not work, it

shouldn't be.   It should be the WANT to express gratitude and

joy by being of service to that person. For example; you love

your baby, so you're happy to feed, change, and nurse your

baby.   It may be early in the morning, but you never get a

resentment of the child.   Relationships are quite similar..nurture

the baby because you brought this love into the world.

Renewing Love.

There are almost 8 billion people on this planet. We can't let relationships that were not for us deter us from finding the person that is! Everyone before your wife was practice. When you meet her, apply all the good stuff you learned and work out all the bad.. that simple.

Pouring Into A Cup.

Not everyone you pour into has the same cup. They are different in size and color. Some people will require you to pour more into them than they can pour back and some might be the same size. Then, some cups are different colors. Some people have different life expectations thus having different cup colors

Be Kind, Rewind.

At times we take for granted the love that we receive. We forget the effort it takes for others to be patient with us, to forgive us, to consider us. The next time you receive an act of kindness, make an effort to give that same effort and more back. Although we can't rewind time, we can still pay it forward.

Growing Love.

If you've been single at times or whether you've been in long relationships, there's always a time that you need to grow and mature in your love life. The way you love has to evolve. Love at an early age may be having long conversations, asking "what are you wearing tomorrow", or buying necklaces with a name on it. While this is fine for young love, once we mature, it may not be the kind of love you want forever. When you're a bit older, love may look like always opening doors, packing your partner's lunch, checking in on your partner. If you checked out a Love Language survey you completed 10 years ago, it might be completely different from your wants and needs today. Allow yourself to mature and allow your love for your next or current partner to mature. Always be aware of how your partner wants to be loved, and ensure you're on a love maturity level that reflects where you are and want to be.

Generally Speaking.

I've heard it often, how bad the dating world is in Atlanta....People are trash, or how things don't meet expectations. The first thing that comes to mind is, "are you seeking great things from a process that only offers generic or general selections?" Then the next thought is, " are you exuding the qualities you want in a mate?" These questions matter and will help you understand who you attract and why you attract them. If you were looking for a t-shirt from your closet and you needed any decent shirt to wear for an activity that might get you dirty, you'd choose a generic t-shirt. Not the cleanest, just whatever is comfortable. A generally decent t-shirt. Does your dating life resemble that process? Are you swiping on an app for someone that just generally fits? Are you meeting people that generally seem okay at the bar? Why aren't you seeking quality? Why aren't you considering qualifications?

Now let's consider what you're exuding? Are there qualities within you that are masked by your physical appearance? Are you a great chef, but only showing your nice body or cute face? Are you a great leader, hiding behind a great car or nice home? You may be inadvertently allowing the outside to shine brighter than what's inside. Thus attracting mostly those seeking the outside because the inside is just a bonus.

Let's start attracting what we really want by being more intentional in our dating. Go after what you want, and show who you are on the inside, outwards.

Building Sandcastles.

If you've ever visited the beach, you've probably built a sandcastle. You can put tons of time into your project, but ultimately poor planning leads to it being washed away. Are you building a home for your heart like this? Are you putting time and effort into a situation that will ultimately wash away because it wasn't built to last?

Attraction is great, but shouldn't be the mainstay of a relationship.   Neither should sex, finance, or other material values. Build based on honesty, respect, loyalty, and values that you truly need.   Remember, anytime your relationship is built on anything less than genuine love and respect, you're only another wave away from disaster.

Love Isn't Convenience.

Often we engage with others in relationships built on how convenient things can be. Typically we base relationships around how easy finances are to attain, or how good sex can be or how little we have to work to get results. Those are conveniences that make relationships easier, not necessarily love.

I often find love in the oddest times and circumstances. When I'm away from my partner, I notice the presence is gone and I don't like that feeling. Or when I'm approaching a new stage in life, I want to share that with my partner. I've looked back over several moments and I've noted that I don't want to 'do life' without my partner. That's how I found love, it was just in the corner of my mind nestling quietly.

Love can't be based on convenient circumstances, because circumstances become inconvenient then challenge your love.

Facts or Feelings.

Relationships require a good balance of factual information and emotional radar. Some things can be quantified, some can't. As human beings, we see patterns because our brains seek patterns. But not all circumstances create patterns, some are just a series of events. That's where logic should come in and play a part. If you've ever met anyone that's dated more than one person, it's a fact that they've "dated around." Doesn't mean they're promiscuous, doesn't mean they're a 'player', just means the first person they dated was not the last. At times we create a narrative based on our experiences, without looking at things from a different perspective. Let's not condemn one another because of facts. It's just information, and what we do with information is everything!

Yokes On You.

We often look for people with similar tastes, interests, and even diets when dating. Those are great dating habits, however, how often do we seek potential mates with similar belief systems? If you're looking to strengthen your relationship with God, why not date someone with the same intent? It's imperative that we put things like this at the forefront of our dating requirements, or the

yoke's (joke's) on you!

Account Overdue.

We've all dated, and some of us are less successful than others.

Not necessarily a bad thing, it happens. And when we're meeting

a new person, we often get curious as to why the last situation

didn't work out.   This conversation is usually where

Accountability is not present. There's an entire rundown of the

relationship of someone else's faults but rarely an Accountability

for our own.   We've gotta start to get clarity on the things we

have done or said that are even minor catalysts to a failure.

Maybe it was a "wandering eye" that caused insecurities within

your relationship? Maybe it's past traumas? We cannot simply portray ourselves as perfect while expecting the next person not

to stumble onto our faults and then fall into the same position.

love, **life,** and language

life.

Life. I see it as a conscious existence. We all have different purposes

in our lives, yet we have purpose.

love, **life,** ^{and} language

Know The Cost.

I've often said that there are extravagant things that I want in my life.

One such item happens to be a Ferrari F8 Spyder. If God were to

grant me the provisions to own that car right now, there are things I

don't understand about it yet, so am I truly ready for it? I may know

how to start it, drive it, and park it…but how much is an oil change,

and where do I get it? How much is a tune up?   How much is

insurance?

We often want things that we don't consider the cost of having. I don't

mean to talk you out of the things you seek, but to ask you to ponder

or seek the costs associated. Really analyze if that person is for you.

Do they exude the traits that you seek? Do you exude the traits that

they seek? Is that house big enough for your family?   Is it too big and

costly for your family?

Knowing the costs puts you in an advantageous position where you're

not surprised about things when/if you do receive them. It's

preparation. It's knowledge. It's wisdom to decide if it's truly what you

seek.

Peace.

We often plan for the future. Whether it be a few hours from now or

years. Honestly, there's no set way to be fully prepared for the future.

We set up 401k accounts to prepare for future bills or retirement, but

what if you're no longer with the company?   That forecast of value

changes dramatically. We choose homes to mortgage and look at

schools in the area to consider great surroundings for our children, but what if life changes everything? How far out should we plan?   Or

should we plan at all. I believe there exists a place where Faith,

Knowledge, and Wisdom meet. That intersection is where having

Faith for God to protect us, doing research to say Knowledge serves

us, and Wisdom to understand that only time dictates good from bad

all join. That alignment becomes Peace.

Peace is being confident that you'll walk across a street safely

knowing you have God's favor; Knowledge that you should be aware

of your surroundings and be careful; while having the Wisdom to

understand that you were exactly where you had to be, whether an

incident occurs or not. Often we stress to change what outcomes may

occur, not realizing we often help those circumstances appear.

Imagine trying to raise children out of poverty, doing illegal acts to

avoid poverty, then your children going into a foster home or poverty

with a relative because you were incarcerated. See how your illegal

acts can create the exact monster you're running from. Gain Peace.

Those children may benefit from living in poverty and become great philanthropists someday.

Stay Humble or Be Humbled.

Sometimes we forget how to be grateful for the many things we have been granted. We lose track of how blessed we are. It's in these moments that we get HUMBLED by life. We go through moments that cause us to take a minute to appreciate what we have and who we are. These moments are not for us to pass by arrogantly as though "we'll easily get past this too", but for us to watch our posture as we do better in treating people and situations in the same manner we would like to be treated.

Places Of Healing.

I've heard people say they don't go to church/temple or have faith because of a bad experience. Usually that experience is with someone who is not quite healed. And I think, we often go to hospitals/clinics for healing, and though we may not come out healed, and we definitely risk coming in contact with sick people and there's a chance of malpractice, we will consistently return AND seek the counsel of other professionals. It is my belief that if we put faith in God as we put faith in Medicine that we'd have a better understanding of our health, our lives, and our purpose…without the bill!

A Matter of Time.

At times we get so caught up in what's currently happening or what just happened that we can't see the goodness coming in the near future. We consider how hard the journey is, but we rarely look forward with hope. We remember how hard it was catching the bus, but we don't get excited enough about the future where we own the bus depot. Let's start looking forward with our hopes and dreams and stay away from the issues that current timing is presenting. It's all just a matter of time.

Where, Not Why.

If you were to take a trip without focusing on where you are, instead of why you made that last turn, you'll surely reach your destination. If you were to focus on that last turn instead of your current position, you'd certainly lose your way, you'll lose focus.

Often we focus on the circumstances and become depressed, angry, and lost. Look up and see where you are in life's journey and be grateful that those turns put you on a better path.

God Positioning System.

Ever asked God for guidance?   If you've ever relinquished control (although you were never really in control) to God, you've been taken on a ride. With That ride comes ups and downs, but you always end up exactly where you're supposed to be. You can't regret the journey or how things went because it's like saying God took you somewhere you weren't supposed to be. God doesn't make mistakes, nor does he miss turns. Life's a trip, take the scenic route!

Best Foot Forward.

Ever felt down and couldn't shake that feeling? Sometimes just making the outside a little more appealing will make the inside that much better. Put that nice pair of shoes on, step into some new clothes, style your hair fresh, put on that winning smile. You'd be surprised at how much better you feel inside from adding a little extra outside!

Staying Enlisted.

How long have you been on your mission or assignment? Has it been months or years since your last promotion or since a change? Sometimes we need to be reminded that we are still on assignment and that we still have a mission to accomplish. It's easy to forget what our purpose is when we've been working so hard for so long. Take a moment to reflect on who you are, what your task is, and how to get there.

Stressing Or Blessing.

Often the way we perceive events dictate whether it was a good or bad experience. We typically allow time to dictate that outcome. And with that, if we allow time to progress, we find that some of our early conceptions are at times opposite to actuality.

I posed the question, "Is the death of a parent a bad thing?" Most would say yes and we can understand why. Now let's say that the parent left a sizable inheritance and was received just at the right time to save the family home. You see how a stressful situation can become a blessing, after time. Now let's say with the remainder, you invested into a worthy cause and quadrupled the amount. Less of a stress, more of a blessing. The construct of time doesn't allow us to see how seemingly bad events lead to some of the most necessary events beforehand, otherwise we'd make the sacrifice required easily. It's in situations like these where Faith comes in. Let's not always count ourselves out, let's learn to rely on God because often he uses seemingly bad situations to shape us for the future.

Ask Permission from God.

Before you begin on any path, ask God if it's for you while praying. Understanding why we may not get the things we want out of life starts with Understanding if we are ready. Only you can answer that truly. Use your recent decisions as a judge.

If you rev your current car hard, don't allow it to 'warm up' properly,

miss regularly scheduled maintenance, always use cheap fuel and

parts, then maybe a new car isn't what you need.

You need better Stewardship lessons..

CHECK YOURSELF.

None of any of this applies if you don't have a healthy conversation

with yourself about your flaws. Telling yourself that "it doesn't matter"

is the best way to fail yourself. The most assured way to failure

begins with the phrase "F#%$ That"

Good Stewardship.

The things that you seek, are you able to take care of them in a way

that honors God and yourself once you have them?

For example; if you're seeking a new car, would you treat a used car

like a new one? Not to idolize or love it, but to care for it in ways that

show you deserved it. Would you drive it so aggressively that you wreck it soon after getting it? Would you hurt others or yourself with it? Would you utilize it to do things you shouldn't do, like attract people so that you can cheat on your spouse?

Be informed, stay informed.

Learn how to conduct research

Take out common words like "and, the, but, if, etc" while using internet search engines.

Subscribe to certain articles based on the quality of the information received.

Don't cut corners with information. Someone can give you information, but not enough for you to think the way they do.   Get the understanding of the information for yourself, then use it. Remember, they can fish for you today and you starve tomorrow, or you can learn to fish today and eat for a lifetime.

Know Your Location.

Where Are You In Your Journey? Take a look at your life and be very serious about your current state. Are you failing to pay bills and debts on time? Are you always late to work or other places? Do you make solid plans?

Where Are You Going? What would you like to fix about your current situation? Would you like to learn to be on time?

You're going to make an assessment of your life one day and sometimes often. Don't rush to finish life, stop and smell the roses. I often dream about the goals I would like to accomplish, then once I have completed those, I begin new ones. Taking the time to live in those accomplishments allows you to have a greater enjoyment of the process. If you push towards the next goal too soon, you'll only be living to 'clear the board' and you'll realize one day, you missed out on life. We often use our phones to document moments only to never really delve into those moments again, but then they're over and we can't get those back. Next time, put the camera away, bask in the moment, store a mental picture.

Life Number.

Count up the total amount of all the things you want; car, home, bills and get an idea of what it may cost you. Keep in mind it needs to be an annual cost. Then divide that total amount into 52. That shows you what you need to make a week to afford it. You can go further by dividing that into 40 to get an idea of what you need to make hourly to afford it. Don't forget to account for requirements like Tithe (10%) and Taxes (depends on your state's income tax for your tax bracket, if applicable. That's what you need to do to accomplish your financial goals.

What's Your Motivation.

What are the reasons you want these things? Is it for someone's attention? Something you've always wanted? Get to the root of WHY?

Allow things in your daily life to motivate you instead of deter you. Sunny days should motivate you to get that new convertible. Rainy days should also motivate you, your thoughts should be, "Days like this I could still drive my convertible, but I wouldn't drop the top."

Discernment.

What Applies To You? Sometimes you get information pouring in from different sources, you should always ask God if the information you received is there to help you or destroy you.

Is this For You? Are the things you want good for you? If you want a fast car, upon getting behind the wheel, would you hurt yourself or others by your actions?

Understand that having a "nothing can stop me" attitude might be an issue. Some roadblocks in life are actually warning signs that this isn't the path for you. You need discernment to know what's for you and what's not.

Looking Back.

Were/Are You Fair/Righteous? Would you say that you deserve good things based on your deeds? Or do you feel you deserve things based on how little you experienced them growing up? There's a major difference. Feeling deserving due to lack does not mean you actually are deserving. It just means you've been deprived.

Giving Back.

Plan to Distribute Knowledge. Are you willing to help others get to your level or beyond you?

Plan to Distribute Wealth. How often are you blessing others with monetary gifts? Are you holding on to every penny?

Learn To Conduct Business Before You Start A Business

You should never take Step 1 without having a plan for Step 10. It's very important to get an entire road map of where you're going before you start the journey. That's where consideration and planning come in. We often find that variables come in and detour our routes and if you've already begun, you'll most likely stop, slow or detour due to issues that you would have planned for. Always allow for buffers. If the budget for outside dining is $100, your budget should include tip amount of 20%, and other tips like valet or parking, and room for extras like dessert or drinks.

Time Management.

Why are you late?

Do not allow yourself to make excuses as to why you were not prepared. Being on time means being ahead of time. Sometimes that comes down to preparing well before time and taking the time to consider adverse circumstances that you cannot control.

For example; you were late to work.

Did you prepare your work attire the previous night?

Was lunch prepared?

Do you have several alarm clocks set as reminders?

Did you get adequate sleep?

Did you start your car ahead of time to allow it to run properly?

Did you communicate with a mate to plan together?

Do you have a checklist of things that you normally take?

These are just examples of things you can do to save time and be

efficient.

Show up like it's the most important day of your life, it just may be!

Level Up.

Treat every challenge like a video game. It doesn't get easier. Bosses

get stronger, enemies keep coming, but for every mission, so do you!

Learn to posture yourself and understand which character you are!

Other's Problems Pressure.

Often others around us, such as spouses or coworkers have

issues/inadequacies that tend to spill out onto us. No one is perfect,

however, not everyone seeks help for their issues and they can and

usually do create pressure for us. For example; if your boss has a deadline for a project and is busy and then delegates it to you, chances are, if there's even a minute issue with said project, it tends to be blown out of proportion. We tend to internalize that pressure and guess what, we pass it on to others. Whether it be a family member, another coworker or simply someone at a fast food restaurant. We often go through situations in our heads over and over, thinking about what we would've said or done differently, or how it made us feel in that moment. That churn of feelings creates a pressure inside, making us a timebomb. It's only so long before we explode, then causing another person to become a "lit fuse".

Circles.

In faith there are unseen circles. Not cliques but outer and inner rings based on amount of faith. The ones in the center being most centered and the outward most circles being to lesser degrees. It often resembles what we have without friends and family, where our most trusted and loved people are closest to our centers. We should all strive to be Inner Circle believers in God, Inner Circle loved ones to our friends and families. Inner Circle coworkers to our peers.

Understand that that Inner position is built on trust, honesty, and knowledge that those next to you are assured to have your best interests at heart at all times.

Tithing IS Gangsta.

Have you ever been "hooked up" with a job or gig or pay opportunity and given the person that set it up, a little appreciation from the funds? That's basically Tithing. Giving God the first 10% of your income, the first of your harvest, the best of your rewards is all Tithing is..it's an appreciation for the opportunity! It's an honor to God for the opportunity you received and profited from. If an artist gets a gig through his manager, he pays up to 22% before he gets his cut!! All that yet we're afraid we can't spare 10% for the God-given talent? We're okay with the government taking a percentage of our pay, often before we see a dime and we're okay with it due to the possibility of a return in some cases…yet we struggle to give God a portion because we can't account for the return. There's the problem. Accounting for the return. We often forget where the opportunity came from and give credit to the wrong source. Remember the source and happily give back!! Keep it gangsta…

Being Honest with Yourself.

How many "little White lies" have you told? How many times have you "stretched the truth"? Do you tell yourself these dishonest things also? Usually… When you lie to yourself you're creating a false perception of what's really happening. And sometime soon, you'll probably begin to believe the lies.

Lying to yourself or anyone else is a sure sign of insecurities and creates dangerous, delusional situations.   Learn to be as honest and respectful as possible. A lot rests on your honesty.

Health IS Wealth.

No matter how much money you attain, no matter how valuable the asset, being unhealthy takes its toll one day. And if you're mentally, spiritually, and physically healthy you're in position to become financially healthy while you're still here. Let's not take good health for granted and we definitely should pay more attention to our health.

Our Mental Health is important, because once you've lost your mind, you're practically of no good to yourself or others. Practice good Healthy Mentality habits often.

Our Spiritual Health is just as important as Mental Health. At times our Spiritual Health can keep us more sound than our Mental Health. There are times when we go through things that we cannot explain, those are the times where a strong Spiritual Health gets us through!

Physical Health cannot be overlooked at all! It's been said that your body is a temple, would you be okay in a place that's falling apart? How comfortable would you be if your home had a roof that was damaged, the stairs weren't stable, and the plumbing didn't work well?

Listen to your body, it talks to you. That's what pain is. We listen intently to pleasure and we seek it more and more. Listen to your body as intently and get rest, good food, and whatever your body needs when it needs it.

Watch For The Signs.

On the road of life, there are signs, just like on the road to anywhere else. And it's very easy to miss or ignore these signs. If you've ever asked God for a sign or discernment regarding a circumstance, the answer is often given like those road signs. You just have to look, and know what to look for. We can't change our path in life no more than we can change the route the highway takes us. We must be comfortable that God paved this way for each of us.

In my personal experiences, I've noticed that there are several signs that conclude a thought, versus one very big and obvious one. I ask for signs and they are answered. And once I see and acknowledge that sign, I'm put at ease, and there is no more struggle.

First, ask for a sign. Then let your concerns go, you can't have fear

and faith. You'll probably try several ways to make changes and

notice none work. That's the sign you asked for. It's worth trying,

but once several different attempts fail while normal circumstances

fail, let go. You have your answer. You don't even have to drive

anymore. You're being guided by your Godly Positioning System.

Know Guidance.

What guides your life? Is it social media? TV? Music? Friends? Is it

religion? Is it Good Nature? I see adults often following trendy ways

they find on social media platforms, and youth being guided by music

they listen to. I also people being Good Samaritans because it's the

right thing to do and religious members integrating Faith into tough

situations. It's very obvious what "guides" those individuals, but do

you know what guides you? Are you aware of what makes you act the

way you do? Take a moment and reflect on your thoughts and

actions. Ask yourself why you do it, what's it for, who is it for? Do this often, and you'll begin to create a picture of who you are. Once that picture becomes clear, ask yourself are you happy with your character?   Know Guidance, know yourself!

Think Like A Boss.

Ready to go on vacation? Ready to have a nice date night? Ready for the new TV? I'm sure all the answers are yes. So, how much do these things cost on an hourly rate based around a 40 hour work week? It puts things in a new perspective to say that you'll have to work 'x' amount of hours to pay for certain expenses. Then you begin to really evaluate if you want or need these things.

Once you decide to get those things on your wishlist, now you have to plan for the extra expenses that come with it. Is there money left in savings? How is everyday life affected by your expenses? If that new expense is a new car, how much is the difference in insurance? Maintenance? Will it require a garage?   Will the new car require any more adjustments to your normal life? Thinking ahead on

this creates the mentality of Thinking Like A Boss.

Watch For The Signs.

When you're living within your purpose, the things you do become

much easier and more pleasant. You no longer toil in your activities.

They become peaceful. Although you still may encounter opposition,

the joy you receive from that work allows you to continue until that

work is done.

Alternatively, when you're living outside your purpose, you seem to

dread that work. You hate going in, you cringe at the thought of it.

Some places you spend time at are simply not for you. Find places

that give you joy, and rest there. This doesn't mean stay in bed all

day and avoid work, it means find something you enjoy doing and do

that.

How You Spend Your Time.

For every instance that you log in to social media, require yourself to spend that equal time doing research on things you're interested in. I specifically scroll Facebook and once I see content that I've seen already, I leave and spend that time seeking information that's useful. There's a saying, "You are what you eat."....but it's more like, "You are what you ingest." The things you watch, listen to and partake in have an effect on you. Put some knowledge in that 'junk food' mix of entertainment you find daily.

Attack of the Drones.

Have you ever stopped and looked at some of the people around you and thought, "they're just living to work, and that's it!" It kinda gives a depressing feeling when you think of so many people that live to work, and that have very little value in their life. We are not meant to be Worker Bees and Drones. We are meant to serve purpose. God has a purpose for us. It's very important that you seek a healthy relationship with God in order to find that purpose! If it's ever occurred to you that you don't want to become a drone, listen to who's on the throne!

Prepare For Testing.

Don't skip the tests that prepare you for upcoming life. You may not understand why you're being tested or what comes after the tests, but be assured that it is only for preparation. That preparation is key to your victory! The testing is always a prelude to future trials. Once you go through the tests, you now prepare to use the lesson for life. It's just like school.

The Disconnect.

At times, it's important that we disconnect from our devices, social media, and even our social circles for brief periods of time. Give ourselves time to refresh and get back grounded or connected to things in our physical world like family and other things. It creates an appreciation for those things that we take for granted.

At the same time, we have to be aware of how much and how long we distance ourselves from others and what the results of that distance mean. Some distance is required when those around you are not those that nurture a positive energy. But we must not mistake "me time" for that. Some people choose "me time", but understand that too much "me time" can be harmful to you. We were not meant to be in solitude.

Do Better.

We have been taught for years that there are times when you just have to suck it up and work harder for things in life. Gotta study harder for better grades, gotta work harder for nicer things…but when was the last time someone told you to be better, simply for the world's sake? Imagine if everyone you knew or met were actively trying to be better people?   Your barista, your banker, your boss? Too many people have the attitude of "take me as I am", while in that same moment, those people wish, want, and pray for better things to enter into their lives….Do better, who knows? You may get better!

Footprints In The Sand.

At times during your life things may seem out of control. You may not understand the how or why, but things seem to work out on their own. You may not reach that financial goal or bills may be abnormally high and upon looking at it, you know you'll fall short, but somehow you didn't. Those are the moments you're being CARRIED. If you've ever read the parable "Footprints In The Sand," then you should understand these moments.

When you find yourself being carried, it's important to first, Give Thanks and Glory. If someone carried you off the battlefield you'd be thankful, show gratitude and give God the proper Glory!

Secondly, Stop Moving. You wouldn't want to fall because you were attempting to move around too much. Only do what you're allowed to do. After receiving resistance when attempting to move, stop. Things won't always make sense or move normally, stop fighting it. Just allow yourself to be carried in that moment.

Finally, when the journey is over, you'll find yourself in places you couldn't have reached by yourself. It's at that moment when most people give thanks to God, but when you've been carried before, you give thanks as soon as you've been picked up because you know the outcome! You'll make leaps and bounds in life. You'll recognize it because doors and pathways open very easily and usually without you attempting much at all. That new place is a blessed one. Don't forget to Tithe to the driver!

Security.

Often during our lives we feel insecure about ourselves. Whether it be from lack or overage. The lack can be from a lack of finance or education or more, while the overage can be from being overweight or other issues. We often allow the imbalance to cause other issues in our relationships. They cause insecurities. At these times, it's most important that we have an understanding of our value. What do people we love value in us? If we've built up a system of value based solely around finances and our finances dwindle then there may be a problem, however, very few occasions are that way.. you should never build a relationship on finance. For the majority of us, our relationships are built on values like honesty, trust, love, partnership and other things that are not so temporary. It's when you recognize YOUR VALUE and how others VALUE YOU that you no longer allow finances or weight to make you insecure. You're much more than a fun date or a flat stomach! You're someone valuable!

love, **life,** and language

Language.

What is the reason for your Communication?

Declarative

To inform-

"Hey, dinner reservations are at 7pm, the address is in the email."

This Communication is designed to give the receptor some type of information. This isn't the sentence we add expressive thoughts into.

We start another sentence after to express our mood.

Interrogative

To question-

"Thanks, are we getting dressed or should we go casual?" This

communication is designed to get answers. Though there may be

information already provided, sometimes there are unanswered

questions that linger.

Exclamatory

To express-

"I'm not feeling up to changing clothes just for dinner." There may or may not be factual information present, because these communications usually express a mood or feeling.

Imperative

To direct-

"Just wear what you have on." This communication gives a directive on what to do. Now, being able to present an idea, directive, question

or concern should be clear to the receptor. How we present things can

largely determine how well they're received and followed.

Look Before You Lecture.

Have you ever been lectured at or had to lecture anyone? It's usually a pretty awkward space for either party. There are usually accusations tossed around, assumptions placed, and they often wind up as tense meetings without a real resolution. One of the very first things that should be addressed in these situations is a question. That question should be, "Why". If no one is taking time to account for why things are occurring, then there can be a perfectly reasonable explanation as to why they are, without all parties understanding. Although there are still times an understanding isn't met, looking before we leap is a great way to assuage painful issues and keep tension to a minimum. The next time you're in a lecture, whether you're being lectured to or doing the lecturing, bring up the "Why" so everyone can gain understanding first.

Out of Control.

Imagine being the captain of a ship and without ever asking or acquiring information, you gave commands to guide the ship…Before long, your crew would see major issues with your leadership! Imagine telling crew members to change direction without knowing exactly where you are….See how that can lead to a disaster. Some of us want Control of situations without actually understanding where things are before sending commands. Even though you're in Command, it shows you're Out of Control. A good leader asks before they assert themselves because they don't want to make foolish decisions that may challenge their leadership capabilities.

Trophies.

Dating and relationships require actual work. They require Work on ourselves to work well with others. It's the best job you'll ever have when LOVE is at the root.   Often in our relationships we seek validation through rewards, Trophies. Often these Trophies can be monetary, gifts, actions, or even nourishment.

One of the best Trophies to receive is Consideration. Consideration goes a very long way. It says that a person values you so much that they go out of their way to think about you when they're planning. Whether it be Consideration for an upcoming meal or a possible road trip, it's valuable.

One of the least valuable Trophies we receive from others is Participation. Have you ever dealt with someone and their response is, "At least I'm dating you." There's something very true about that statement, "at least". Which says, "you're not very valuable to me, and I may be doing you a favor." There are no Participation Trophies awarded in relationships. No one wants anyone around because they're a living, breathing person. Don't go on a date that you don't want because you said you'd go, then resent going and thus making the date terrible. Don't do anything in any type of relationship from pity or a feeling of obligation. Do it from the heart.

Shhh, Don't Tell Nobody.

Some things that are revealed to you aren't meant for everyone to know just yet. Some things that God whispers aren't meant for everyone's ears. We get anxious and want to share our plans and ideas with everyone close to us, but at times they aren't ready for what you're about to give them. Ask for discernment regarding things you've been told. You don't feed a newborn steak, they're not ready to receive it yet. It's baby food until they are developed enough.

Re-Defining.

Words come already defined. And although some words have negative or positive connotations, if that word applies to you I'm someway, you can't run from the connotation, you can't redefine the word. I've heard people say, "This is MY TRUTH". Truth is truth, you can't reshape it for your narrative. Otherwise it's a lie. I've heard people say, "I'm not selfish, I'm focused on my journey"...it sounds so much nicer, yet it's the same thing. Be aware of yourself, even when it paints a picture that's not what you want. It allows a real snapshot of your life and an amazing opportunity for you to fix it.

Ghosting.

In today's society, the term "Ghosting" refers to killing communication, typically without notice. Ghosting usually leaves one party lost about the outcome of communication and creates an unhealthy situation, while the party that starts the Ghosting shrugs the other party off as if they don't exist. Ghosting can have disastrous effects, not everyone is comfortable with being ghosted. And at times, the party that Ghosts can regret ever committing the act later.

Healthy communication Is a key to Healthy living. Instead of Ghosting someone, commit to explaining why you're ending communication. It's much healthier for all parties. It gives the other party a reason to consider actions, thoughts, or words they've used, and possibly correct it. It serves the disconnecting party with a way to end communication without negative repercussions. And it possibly leads to a solution that works for all parties.

Positive Expectations.

Times where you communicate, "Good morning", or "Thanks" you typically expect that same energy returned. At times you may be low in energy and receive an unexpected high-energy response. Or vice versa. It's not always that we receive high-energy responses. It may be because that person is in deep thought, or a concerned state, maybe even depression. It's at those times that we return an even higher energy response. You don't fight negative with negative, only positive energy. Learn to love yourself and the world around you so much that a negative response is something you'd like to clean up versus fight, not all fights are for you. Respond with a loving response. Don't just wait for it, create a place for Positive Expectations.

Microwaveable Miracles.

I've yet to see a meal that comes from a microwave that's anywhere as nutritious or close to the taste of a completely cooked meal. That's why we wait for what's better. Microwaveable food is okay when we're on the move, but we know for a fact that the food lacks the nutritional value we need to grow as we should. The only benefit is a quick fill of our stomachs.

Have you ever needed a miracle? Have you been in need of quick funds or fast healing? You wanted a microwavable miracle. God saw fit that you get the slow-cooked meal though, and it was definitely better for your growth!

The hardest lesson to learn is that growth, which is hard, takes time! Don't settle for quick snacks when the best thing for you is the slow-cooked meal!

Effective Communication.

Are you an effective communicator? It's not shouting or yelling. A lot of communication can be effectively sent if you take the time to understand what you're trying to convey, who you're conveying to, and what purpose.

Imagine asking a child to get prepared for the day while you're busy doing the same. Knowing that child, can you guarantee that child will efficiently do the things you'd like them to do without having direction, structured time, or assistance? Usually they lack all three. So when you ask, are you giving grace to that child or are you yelling moments later for a failure that your Communication caused? Knowing that you should structure your requests based on priority, time, and other parameters could give you an edge on getting things done.

For Example; "Hey, (child) I need you to brush your teeth, put on your socks then shoes, and meet me at the breakfast table in 10 minutes."

Now you've given a few tasks some structure and not overwhelmed the child. There was also a time expectation and even a priority with what you asked first and last. Effective..

Perception and Reality.

The saying goes, "Perception IS Reality." Meaning you can believe a circumstance happened a way, and until there are facts to debunk or support your perception, it's pretty much going to remain as your belief. Often when we communicate to others, if there are no

witnesses or recordings, we don't always know how we are received

by others. I witnessed an argument recently between a man and a

woman where the woman abruptly interrupted a separate group

conversation to speak with a man. The fellow asked if something was

wrong, and the woman immediately became defensive and asked,

"why would you think something is wrong, what did you do?"

This turned into a debate based around the woman not being

considerate of her role and immediately placing the blame on the man,

and his defensive state of mind. Her perception was that she simply

approached and made a request. His perception was that she

accused him of wrongdoing. From a third perspective, I noticed she

approached without regard to his ongoing conversation, he didn't

notice her presence because she walked in behind him, her body

language and tone suggested there was an issue, and his vulnerable

state put him on defense. The reality is a blend of both. Neither

perception was spot-on. We have to be able to recognize our faults

within communication to effectively communicate with others. Take

the time out to review misunderstandings calmly. I often say that the truth is 3-fold; the first perspective, the second perspective, and what actually happened.

Curse Words.

Have you ever wondered, "Why is foul language called Curse Words?" Well, because cursing as an offense comes from throwing a curse or an evil spell. Morphology and etymology are two examples of the studies of the history and breakdown of work meanings.

Take a moment before you decide to formulate that sentence and be sure you're not sending out more than you mean. Your last words could haunt you.

Define Your Support.

I've often heard people ask, demand, and cry for support. I hear people create distance between themselves and others over support.

At times I've even questioned, What does SUPPORT look like? Is support a financial investment? Is it a hug or a vent session? Is it a person accompanying you on a task? We must first define what support looks like before we ask anyone to support. Once defined, we then can't expect the person to agree to that support, we can only ask. If granted, support may come in a form that may not supply the complete need, but may be a substantial start. Let's not be defeated by a lack of support. The amount you receive may be all you actually need to get your task completed. Let's not create a NEW battle because the people we choose to help can't help us win completely. Sometimes the battle is YOUR personal challenge to overcome.

Talk Em Up.

Every time you hear a friend or relative talk about things they want to accomplish, speak encouragement into their endeavors. Be that person that gives them the belief that they can make it happen, there are plenty of people working against them, often without knowing it. We need that word from those around us.

Often we give up on those around us but it's important to be a 'constant gardener' and to remind ourselves that not all LIVING THINGS grow at the same rate.

With That being said, be aware of DEAD THINGS. People are not dead things, only works that don't bear good fruit. Those fruits should be to God's glory and if not, they are considered Dead Works. Even in the dictionary Dead Works are considered to be tasks that are fruitless.

Speak life into those you value and ensure they consider thoughtfully who gets credit from their duty.

Know Your Audience.

Have you ever wanted to tell your friend or family about an idea or joke or thought? I'm sure you have. And at times it's met with anger or reception, even from the same person! Know Your Audience! At times, the people you communicate with aren't in a space where your thoughts can be correctly conveyed without trouble. Children are pretty good at this thought. They'll often try to understand a parent's mood before they say they got in trouble or before they ask for a toy. Let's not manipulate the situation, but rather understand the timing means a lot. And with good timing, just like any good joke, we can get our point across without issue.

Marry A Mindreader.

Often we don't communicate our feelings to those close to us. We have an expectation that since they know things about us; favorite foods, music, clothes, etc., that they're also supposed to know what we feel or think. We have to be better at communicating exactly what

we mean, and one of the first steps is to be sure internally.

Is this what I really feel?

Is this realistic?

What type of reaction am I expecting?

We must also be aware of the non-verbal communication we send.

Are you asking for money with your hand out? Are you giving a

directive and pointing with your finger? We use our body language at

times without regard to how it makes others feel or the perception.

Body language can greatly alter the message.

A fun way to work on communication with others is to make 'hard-to-

talk-about' topics a little more cool and less edgy. Use phrases that all

parties included aren't offended by and begin to establish a bridge of

communication. Creation of these phrases or words can open up

speaking points if done correctly. Just remember to be polite,

understanding, non-aggressive, and fun.

Check Your Account.

How often do you account for your part in issues? How often do you tell others while in an argument what you know you're accountable for. That simple honesty could be the resolution to the conflict. At times we are the reason for our conflicts, and sometimes it's a joint debacle. I've often seen that missed communication is the culprit.

Imagine having a joint account. If you are about to make a purchase, it's always a good practice to check your account, and even after that purchase. It's important to know exactly what's going on with that account before decisions are made. Your relationship is an account just like a bank account. Its currency is Love. Before you make any decisions with that account that your partner is tied to, ensure you have proper communication as available credit, good love as an available balance, and accountability as a correct updated ledger before blaming your partner for overspending. Not checking YOUR accountability can lead to minor overages that eventually close the account. Examine what you did wrong, admit to what you did wrong,

make things right.

Playing Games/Manipulation.

One of the most dangerous things we can do with other people is

attempt to manipulate. We call that "playing games" at times..

It's the process of changing words/actions/thoughts etc., around to get

a desired outcome. No one likes it, yet we do it in hopes of protecting

ourselves, then lie to ourselves to say it's to protect others.

If you've ever lied so that a relationship could continue, you're guilty

of this too. We all have done something like this to preserve a

relationship or friendship, but the outcome is usually worse. Most

times the victim says, "you could've just told me!" It's then that we find

that our reason for the manipulation was unnecessary AND exactly

how dangerous it was. Often circumstances turn out better when you're honest and you accept the outcome without trying to

manipulate certain aspects.